INVEST FIRST, INVESTIGATE LATER

INVEST FIRST, INVESTIGATE LATER

And 23 Other Trading Secrets of George Soros, the Legendary Investor

Robert Slater

IRWIN
Professional Publishing®

Chicago • London • Singapore

This publication is designed to provide accurate and authoritative information in regard to the subject matter covered. It is sold with the understanding that neither the author nor the publisher is engaged in rendering legal, accounting, or other professional service. If legal advice or other expert assistance is required, the services of a competent professional person should be sought.

From a Declaration of Principles jointly adopted by a Committee of the American Bar Association and a Committee of Publishers.

Times Mirror
Higher Education Group

Library of Congress Cataloging-in-Publication Data

Slater, Robert, 1943–

     Invest first, investigate later : And 23 other trading secrets of George Soros, the legendary investor / Robert Slater.

        p. cm.

     Includes index.

     ISBN 0-7863-0994-6

     1. Investments. 2. Investment analysis. 3. Soros, George—Knowledge—Investments.   I. Title.

HG4521.S618   1997

332.6—dc20   96–13011

Printed in the United States of America

1 2 3 4 5 6 7 8 9 0 QBP 3 2 1 0 9 8 7 6

CONTENTS

Introducing Super Investor
George Soros

Until the fall of 1992 few people outside the world of high finance had heard of George Soros. Today, he is considered a business superstar, known as the man who "beat the Bank of England," earning nearly $1 billion overnight when he guessed correctly that Great Britain would devalue the pound. Soros also has a reputation as a man who moves financial markets, and while some doubters don't believe that one man, even George Soros, can alone influence the markets, enough people believe in Soros's powers to give him legendary status.

What is indisputable is that Soros ranks as the world's greatest investor. No one else has performed as effectively for so long in the financial markets as the Budapest-born Soros. Beginning in 1969, when he established his Quantum Fund, Soros has produced an incredible investment record. A mere $1,000 invested in Quantum back in 1969 would have swollen to $2,150,000 by 1995 had dividends been reinvested. His success has induced many on Wall Street and in the City in London to aspire to be "like George Soros" and to discover George's trading secrets.

Invest First, Investigate Later: & 23 Other Trading Secrets of George Soros, the Legendary Investor provides a look at Soros's trading secrets. Many of those secrets are as applicable for the small investor as they are for someone like George Soros. Learning Soros's secrets will not guarantee that the reader will make $1 billion overnight, but by catching a glimpse of the way he works, the reader can acquire some sense of how to read the financial markets more carefully and more accurately.

There is no better teacher than George Soros. Soros's record since 1969 represents a compound growth rate of 35 percent, the best in the business. Had Soros achieved this kind of return with a $50 to $100 million fund, the feat would have been impressive. But to have done so with a multibillion-dollar portfolio has made Wall Street stand up and take notice. Soros's most spectacular year was 1993, when he personally earned a record-breaking $1.1 billion, a larger sum than any American had ever earned in a single year, and his Quantum Fund gained 61.5 percent. In only one year—1981—did Soros's fund show a loss. The fund also had a tough year in 1994, showing a lukewarm 3.9 percent return, but he did markedly better that year than other hedge funds, some of which fell as much as 30 percent. The year 1995 was a better one for the Soros fund, up 24 percent as of September.

Quantum is one of the first offshore funds (offshore of the United States, that is) freely available to non-American investors. This is in contrast to other offshore funds, which are limited by American law to 99 investors and which ordinarily required a minimum investment of at least $1 million. It is also the most successful of the relatively new breed of hedge funds, those highly secretive, esoteric partnerships of rich people who allow money managers like Soros to take incredible risks with their money in order to get even richer. To qualify as a member of the Quantum Fund, an investor needs to pony up a minimum of $1 million.

Soros was born into an upper-middle-class Jewish family in 1930. During 1944, the year that the Nazis occupied Budapest, Hungary, he moved from one hiding place to another to avoid detection. Had the Nazis caught him and discovered that he was a Jew, they would have killed him. After the war, Soros left Hungary on his own for London, where he studied economics at the London School of Economics, graduating in 1952. He saw himself as a philosopher in the making, but, after a few years of apprenticing with British firms in the securities field, he journeyed to New York, where he sold European securities at various brokerage firms, including F. M. Mayer, Wertheim & Co., and Arnhold & S. Bleichroeder.

At the latter firm, Soros teamed up with a young Yale graduate from Alabama, James B. Rogers Jr., to start the Quantum Fund. Soros's forte was sensing sound investment ideas; starting with $250,000 in 1970, the fund grew to $381 million a decade later, and Soros's personal wealth by then was estimated at $100 million.

When hedge funds began years earlier, a small group of managers adopted a strategy of buying some stocks and selling others short. These funds were "hedged" because their portfolios were divided between stocks that would profit if the market rose and short positions that would profit if stocks fell.

Soros and a number of other hedge fund kings abandoned that strategy and moved beyond the U.S. stock market, betting on broad global shifts in stock markets, interest rates, and currencies. Rather than bet just on stocks, they were betting increasingly on the overall direction of financial markets. On an average trading day, Soros's funds were buying and selling $750 million of securities. The fund sells short, uses complex financial instruments, and borrows large quantities of money—tools largely unavailable to average investors.

According to most reports, Soros owned one-third of the Quantum Funds. But for all of his financial success in the 1970s and 1980s, he remained a mysterious figure, partly because, like so many others on Wall Street, he genuinely believed that publicity was poison to an investor. Then along came an event that suddenly turned Soros into a business celebrity. It happened in September 1992, when he shrewdly sensed that Britain's mounting economic doldrums would force it to devalue the pound. He took a position of $10 billion, much of that from his fund, the rest from loans, on the premise that Britain would have to devalue. When it did on September 15, 1992, Soros earned nearly $1 billion.

Knowledge of Soros's coup took time to seep out to the public, but when it did in late October, he became an overnight superstar. "I Made a Billion As the Pound Crashed" was the front-page headline written in huge, black, bold letters in London's *Daily Mail*. The media could not get enough of Soros. He had made "the fastest billion in history," as one newspaper put it. Fleet Street dubbed him "The Man Who Broke the Bank of England." Even had he wished to, Soros was unable to crawl back into his shell. He had made a larger sum in one day than most individuals see in a thousand lifetimes. His September coup helped put him at the head of the annual list of *Financial World*'s best-paid figures on Wall Street for 1992: by earning $650 million that year, Soros outdid junk bond king Michael Milken's 1987 record of $550 million.

From time to time, George Soros has talked about his investment strategies and investment style. Often he talks in generalities, refusing to get into specifics, fearing that he might give away some exceptionally secret and useful device for making large sums. Yet he has provided enough of a road map for us to describe how he invests, how he makes decisions, what strategies seem to work for him.

Here, then, in a nutshell are the 24 trading secrets Super Investor George Soros employs.

INVESTMENT SECRET

Your View of Reality Is Distorted

To understand how George Soros operates in the financial markets, one must come to grips with his philosophical views.

Since he was a student in London in the early 1950s, Soros has been interested in the questions that philosophers ask: How does the world work? How can we understand its workings? Is such knowledge even attainable? Soros asks those questions because in his early days he had genuine aspirations to become a philosopher—not to make a lot of money.

Many people ask the same questions. What is life all about? Why am I here? How do things work—the big things like the Universe, the Brain, Humankind? Most people ponder such questions for a brief moment or two, then move on to other more practical issues such as making a living or raising a family. They leave the big questions to philosophers, believing the answers to be largely elusive.

Soros, though, wanted to be a philosopher. He was eager to try to come up with answers to these questions. It's no surprise that he was prepared to probe such weighty matters, for as a child, George actually thought of himself a kind of god, with all the grand implications that such professions of divinity suggested. By the time he was a college student, it was easy for him to fall under the spell of philosophy professors who dwelt on the questions he cared most about. It took little encouragement on their part to produce in him a burning desire to develop a grand philosophical scheme.

Such a scheme might have benefited humanity; if accepted by the world at large, it might even have benefited George Soros. But when he philosophized in his early days, Soros had no ambitions of making a fortune. At first he saw no connection between the world of philosophy and the world of high finance. He simply wanted to advance human knowledge. To Soros, the only way to accomplish that noble goal was to begin with the most fundamental questions of humankind—to probe one's existence. He quickly identified his own understanding of existence as the main problem in attaining knowledge of one's existence.

Before he got very far, Soros came to a dramatic conclusion: that the task of unraveling the mysteries of life was nearly impossible. For one simple reason: He believed that to even begin to study who or what we are and how we know anything about existence, we have to be able to look at ourselves objectively. The trouble is that we cannot.

Soros concluded—and that conclusion plays a central role in both his philosophy and his attitudes about the financial markets—that what we think is inextricably tied up in what we think *about*. Accordingly, it is not possible for our thinking process to possess some independent reference point by which to judge or come to understand existence.

Unable to achieve this independent point of reference, people cannot, in effect, get out of their skins, cannot look at the world through undistorted prisms. Thus, the idea that perfect knowledge is attainable is at best questionable, as Soros suggests, for anytime one tries to understand a situation in which one participates, that understanding does not add up to knowledge. In the early 1950s Soros decided that essentially all of our perceptions of the world—that is, our search for what existence is all about—are flawed or distorted.

Soros then deduced that, given the limits of human knowledge, the only practical thing for him to do—and it was this deduction that is central to his financial strategies—was to focus on the significance of these distorted or flawed perceptions in shaping all sorts of events.

INVESTMENT SECRET

Take Market Expectations into Account

Classical economic theory has long believed in the concept of equilibrium. From this concept economic theorists have postulated the notion of perfect competition, which suggests that under certain circumstances self-interest, if left unrestrained, leads to the optimal allocation of resources. Equilibrium occurs when all firms produce at a point where marginal costs are the same as the market price, and when every consumer purchases a quantity whose marginal utility is the same as the market price. The assumption is that everyone will benefit as long as neither buyer nor seller influences the market price.

Equilibrium, though, says George Soros, is not observed in real life, certainly not in the financial markets, where market prices fluctuate a great deal, so the notion of perfect competition is flawed. It assumes perfect knowledge, and that is not possible, says Soros, "because understanding a situation in which one participates cannot qualify as knowledge." He questions modern economic theories that argue that the main task of economics is to study the relationship between supply and demand but not to study supply and demand by themselves. He also questions the assumption of these economists that the demand and supply curves should be taken as given. That assumes—incorrectly, Soros insists—that participants who are supposed to choose between alternatives in accordance with their scale of preferences can know what those preferences and alternatives are. The shape of the supply and demand curves, says Soros, cannot be assumed to be given, since both incorporate the expectations of the participants regarding events that are shaped by those very expectations.

When investors look at the financial markets, expectations play a large role. The decision to purchase and sell something is based upon the expectation of what that price will be in the future; future prices depend on the decisions that are made at the present time about buying and selling. So, says Soros, one cannot assume that supply and demand are determined only by outside forces that are independent of the expectations of participants.

It may seem absurd for anyone who believes in classical economic theory to accept the idea that events in the marketplace are going to affect supply and demand, because students of classical economic theory accept that the shape of the supply and demand curves determines the market price. But Soros believes that supply and demand are subject to the influences of the market—and that results in fluctuating prices, not equilibrium.

Says Soros: "Anyone who trades in markets where prices are continuously changing knows that participants are very much influenced by market developments." Not only do rising prices attract buyers; buying itself contributes to rising prices, resulting in a self-reinforcing trend. There could not be any self-reinforcing trends if supply and demand were based on factors that had nothing to do with market prices.

Soros says that this kind of paradoxical behavior characterizes all financial markets, which serve as discounting mechanisms for future developments. The stock market is a good example, as are foreign exchange markets, banking, and any form of credit. In short, says Soros, "Market developments dictate the evolution of the conditions of supply and demand, not the other way around."

INVESTMENT SECRET

Markets Aren't Efficient

While he clung to the idea of being a philosopher, George Soros knew that he had to make a living, so he became a financial analyst. He realized that, aside from providing him with an income, the financial world could serve as a kind of laboratory for his theories. If he could show that his theories were valid in a financial context, he might be able to demonstrate that they had general validity as well.

His goal was to determine whether there was any validity to the notion that all perceptions are flawed and distorted. He then made what one might call a leap of faith by asserting that in effect people viewed the financial markets through a set of lenses that were distorted. Essentially, Soros asked himself: Is this theory a good way to determine how financial markets work?

Soros knew well that such thoughts ran counter to the prevailing wisdom among market analysts. Those analysts, proponents of the efficient-market theory, are predisposed to think that there is logic or rationality to market operations. They are bolstered in their thinking by classical economics, which teaches that financial markets move toward a state of equilibrium. Because markets reach equilibrium, it is possible to assume that perfect knowledge and perfect competition are attainable.

In effect, proponents of the efficient-market theory believe that it is possible, given the right tools of analysis and access to the right information, to make predictions about the markets that would stand up. They build their theories on two premises: that one can acquire a perfect understanding of the financial markets at any given time and that stock prices reflect all available information.

Believing the markets operate on the basis of logic is comforting to these people. It is too disquieting, too nerve-racking, not to mention too risk-laden, to think otherwise when dealing in the market. It is a good feeling to believe that with enough hard work, the proper analysis, and access to the right sources, one can guess accurately how stock prices will behave. These rationalists argue that because investors can acquire perfect knowledge of a company, every share is valued at precisely the correct price. That is, the price of every share is the outcome of a rational set of calculations that, if done correctly, results in the "correct" price, in much the same way one solves a mathematical problem. The efficient-market school assumes that anyone following these rules will, when confronted with the available choice of stocks, select the best ones. Share prices will remain anchored—or rationally related—to the estimates of a company's future earnings.

This efficient-market hypothesis sounds simple; its very simplicity makes it one of the most popular theories of how the stock market works. To George Soros it was not just too simple. It was plain wrong.

In adopting a contrarian view of the way financial markets operate, Soros hoped to provide evidence for his conviction that the world was hardly rational, that it was impossible to attain perfect understanding of anything, including the financial markets—in short, that all those analysts are wrong in their view of what made stock prices rise or fall.

INVESTMENT SECRET

Look for Big Discrepancies between Perceptions and Actual Events

Soros applies a different set of assumptions to the way the financial markets operate.

The first is that there is nothing rational or logical about their operations. If, as he posits, all our perceptions are distorted or flawed, there is no way to attain perfect understanding of the markets, no way to acquire perfect information that might aid in figuring out stock prices.

In the real world, he insists, people can attain only an imperfect understanding of things. Soros wrote:

> The major insight I bring to understanding things in general is the role that imperfect understanding plays in shaping events. Traditional economics is based on theories of equilibrium, where supply and demand are equal. But if you realize what an important role our imperfect understanding plays, you realize that what you are dealing with is disequilibrium.

In the real world, he maintains, the decision to buy or sell a stock—or anything else—is based not on the ideal of equilibrium in the financial markets but rather on the notion that markets are in a state of disequilibrium. If there were equilibrium, Soros asks, why do market prices fluctuate, presumably without any perceived degree of logic? Because participants in the financial markets have biases, there can be no equilibrium. In Soros's view, one cannot posit equilibrium because one's bias is always caught up in the act of moving toward that equilibrium, and since biases may shift in the process, it's not possible to fix on one "target."

Financial markets function in a state of disequilibrium, and there will always be discrepancies between the perceptions of the participants and actual events. When the discrepancy is negligible, it's not worth worrying about, for it does not change participants' perceptions. When it is large, the discrepancy needs to be taken into account, for it does change those perceptions.

INVESTMENT SECRET

See the Link between People and Events

Those who assume that economic life is rational and logical argue as well that there are no discrepancies in the financial markets—that the markets are always going to be "right": Right in the sense that market prices tend to discount—or take into account—future developments, even when those developments are unclear. Most investors believe that they can discount what the market will do in the future, that is, take future developments into account in advance.

To Soros this was impossible. To him, "Any idea of what the future will be like is by definition going to be biased and partial. I don't mean that facts and beliefs exist autonomously. On the contrary, what I have argued in expounding the theory of reflexivity is that *what beliefs do is alter facts.*"

In effect, then, market prices are not going to be right, for they always ignore the influences that can and will come from future developments. Market prices are always going to be "wrong" because they offer, not a rational view of the future, but a biased one.

"But distortion works in both directions," contends Soros. "Not only do market participants operate with a bias, but their bias can also influence the course of events. This may create the impression that markets anticipate future developments accurately, but in fact it is not present expectations that correspond to future events but future events that are shaped by present expectations. The participants' perceptions are inherently flawed, and there is a two-way connection between flawed perceptions and the actual course of events, which results in a lack of correspondence between the two. I call this two-way connection *'reflexivity.'*"

Soros is convinced that what explains the behavior of financial markets is not the efficient-market hypothesis but a reflexive relationship between the biases of investors and the actual course of events, another phrase for the economic fundamentals of firms.

INVESTMENT SECRET

Uncover Market Biases

Markets are inherently unstable. What causes market instability are our perceptions. More precisely, our biased or flawed perceptions.

According to George Soros, the "bias" of investors toward a stock, whether positive or negative, causes the price to rise or fall. That bias operates as a *"self-reinforcing factor,"* which then interacts with "underlying trends" to affect investor expectations. The price of a stock is determined not by incisive reaction to attainable information but rather by perceptions that are as much the outcome of emotions as of hard data. The resulting price movement might lead management to repurchase shares or enter upon a merger, acquisition, or buyout, thus influencing the fundamentals of the stock.

Soros's theory embraces the notion that the prices investors pay are not simply passive reflections of value; rather, they are active ingredients in creating a valuation of the stock. This two-way feedback between perception and reality—what Soros calls reflexivity—forms a key to his theory.

To develop a sound economic theory, one needs to ascertain the "facts." However, as Soros notes, "When events have thinking participants, the subject matter is no longer confined to facts but also includes the participants' perceptions. The chain of causation does not lead directly from fact to fact but from fact to perception and from perception to fact."

A second key to Soros's theory is the role played by misconceptions or biases in shaping events. When he talks about misconceptions, he really means a discrepancy between the perceptions of the participants and the outcome of events. Participants in financial markets cannot confine their thoughts just to facts. Rather, they have to take into account the thoughts of every participant—themselves included. Because the thinking of the participants does not correspond to the facts, there is uncertainty. Because of this uncertainty, almost always one finds a discrepancy—not a correspondence—between the perceptions of the participants and the outcome. The discrepancy is another word for misconceptions or mistakes.

Misconceptions, or, as he sometimes calls them, divergences between a participant's thinking and the actual state of affairs, are always there. Sometimes, the divergence is small and it can correct itself. He calls this situation near-equilibrium. Sometimes, the divergence is large and not self-correcting. This situation he terms far-from-equilibrium.

When the divergence is large, perception and reality are far removed from one another. No mechanism exists to bring them closer together. Indeed, forces are at play tending to keep them far apart. These far-from-equilibrium situations take one of two forms.

At one extreme, even though perceptions and reality are far apart, the situation is stable. Stability is of no interest to Soros the investor. At the other extreme, the situation is unstable and events move so quickly that the participants' views cannot keep up with them. Instability is of extreme interest to Soros.

7

INVESTMENT SECRET

Capitalize on Instability

For reflexivity to become noticeable, at first it has to at least be self-reinforcing. If a self-reinforcing process occurs over a long enough period, it has to become unsustainable, since either the gap between thinking and reality becomes too large or the bias of the participants becomes too pronounced.

When the gap between perception and reality is wide, events often run out of control, a situation found typically in *boom/bust sequences* in the financial markets. Soros thinks of these sequences as manias, "processes which are initially self-reinforcing but unsustainable and therefore eventually have to be reversed."

The potential always exists for such boom/bust sequences. Soros holds that boom/bust sequences are prone to develop because markets are always in a state of flux and uncertainty. The way to make money is to look for ways to capitalize on that instability, to search for the unexpected developments.

The hard part, of course, is identifying a boom/bust sequence. To identify one, the investor has to understand how other investors are perceiving the various economic fundamentals. Determining what the market—the sum total of these investors—thinks at any given moment is the essence of Soros's investment technique. Once an investor knows what the "market" is thinking, it becomes possible to jump the other way, to bet on the unexpected event, to bet that a boom/bust cycle is about to happen or has already begun.

How, though, does a boom/bust sequence take hold?

When he appeared before the House Banking Committee on April 13, 1994, Soros provided a brief explanation, suggesting that he disagreed with the "prevailing wisdom." While most believed that financial markets tended toward equilibrium and discounted the future accurately, Soros assumed that "financial markets cannot possibly discount the future correctly because they do not merely discount the future: they help to shape it."

Sometimes, he said, financial markets might *affect* the fundamentals even though they are supposed to *reflect* them. "When that happens, markets enter into a state of dynamic disequilibrium, and behave quite differently from what would be considered normal by the theory of efficient markets."

Such boom/bust sequences do not occur frequently. When they do, because they influence the economy's fundamentals, they are disruptive. A boom/bust sequence can happen only when a market is dominated by trend-following behavior. "By trend-following behavior, I mean people buying in response to a rise in prices and selling in response to a fall in prices in a self-reinforcing manner. Lopsided trend-following behavior is necessary to produce a violent market crash, but it is not sufficient to bring it about."

A key question for Soros—and for all of us—is: What generates trend-following behavior?

INVESTMENT SECRET

Discern Chaos

At 5:30 P.M., September 15, 1992, George Soros was sitting in his office on the 33rd floor of a midtown Manhattan skyscraper. He was focusing on western Europe. He had been following developments in the European Economic Community for the past few years, sensing that events there were leading to a financial explosion.

That day Soros was testing his theory on the entire European financial world. He dismissed all those investors who believed the financial markets to be rational, that stock prices had a built-in logic. He scoffed at their conviction that all one had to do was discern that logic, and one would become rich. To Soros, the financial world was unstable and chaotic. The trick was to discern the chaos; only then was it possible to become rich. There were no mathematical formulas that, once solved, would explain how stock prices were going to perform. The stock market operated on the basis not of logic but psychology, Soros suggested. More precisely, the herd instinct.

For Soros to discover whether his theories would help him in any given situation in the markets, he first had to figure out "where the market was going," that is, when and how the herd was going to get behind a certain stock, currency, or commodity. He had been applying that theory to the European financial world for the past few years, laying back, waiting for the timing to be right to strike, waiting for the herd instinct to take over. When it did, he would be ready to pounce, ready to seize the opportunity if it arose. This time, he was sure he was right. And this time, he was ready to place the biggest bet anyone had ever made in the investment world. If he lost, he would surely lose some money. He had lost money before, though. During the October 1987 stock market crash, he had read things wrong and had to cut his losses, about $300 million.

But more often, he had won money—for his elite group of clients—and he had done it so well and so continuously that he had already been called by *Institutional Investor* magazine in June 1981 "the World's Greatest Money Manager."

In his office late that September day Soros wished he were in London, where it was only 10:30 A.M. That was where the action was. A look of satisfaction crossed Soros's face as he thought back to November 9, 1989, the crucial day when the Berlin Wall came tumbling down. Everyone knew how significant an event the dismantling of the wall was for modern history.

Others believed, or at least they hoped, that with the end of the Berlin Wall and the eventual reunification of West and East Germany, a new unified Germany would arise and prosper. As he often did, Soros thought differently. He sensed that the Germans would have a hard time economically trying to unify the two countries into one large Germany. He also sensed that Germany would turn inward, worry about its own economic problems, and not consider it important to help other western European countries get out of their economic doldrums.

Soros believed that an inward-looking Germany would have vast implications for the economies—and the currencies—of the other countries in Europe. He watched and waited. In 1990, he had watched Great Britain take the fateful step of joining forces with the new monetary system that had been set up for western European countries, the ERM, or Exchange Rate Mechanism. Soros thought it had been a mistake for Britain to participate, for membership was too confining, too restrictive; it tied Britain's hands and could keep it from taking the bold steps necessary to resolve its own economic problems.

The British economy was not strong, and by joining the ERM, it was essentially linking itself to the strongest

economic power in western Europe—the new united Germany—a linkage that would make Britain ultimately dependent upon the Germans, for the Germans, because they were
the strongest economy in the region, essentially dictated if
and when other European countries could raise or lower
interest rates, devalue currencies, and so on.

That dependence upon Germany, thought Soros, would
eventually prove fatal for the British. Britain might want to
change its monetary policies, and it would not be able to.
It would have to link those policies with the monetary policies of a more dominant Germany.

Just as Soros had predicted, 1992 brought a financial
crisis to western Europe. The British and other western
European countries with sagging economies wanted to
lower their interest rates. The Germans, however, were
unwilling to reduce their interest rates for their own domestic reasons: They were deeply afraid that inflation would
recur. They remembered with horror the 1920s, when inflation was the poison that brought the German economy to
collapse. If the Germans would not lower their rates, the
other European nations would lose whatever benefits
accrued to lowering theirs. By dropping their interest rates,
other European countries would stand in jeopardy of weak-
ening their currencies, and their weakened currencies would
be prey to speculators. So Britain was increasingly stuck.

Its economy was getting worse and worse. The overvalued pound was under increasing pressure. To improve
its economy, Britain needed to reduce the value of the pound,
which would make its exports more attractive. But ERM
rules forced Britain to keep the pound pegged at 2.95 to the
German mark. Over the summer of 1992, British political
leaders had insisted that they would survive the storm, that

there would be no devaluation of the pound. Britain would not break ranks with the ERM.

Somehow, they would muddle through. Nonsense, thought George Soros, who understood how dire Britain's economic situation was. There was no way the British would be able to remain in the ERM. They would have to abandon ship. He discerned the chaos in the situation. And he thought about getting rich.

The crisis began in mid-September. Rumors began floating that the Italian lire would be devalued. Traders in New York began selling lire out of fear of a devaluation. On Sunday, September 13, the lire was devalued by 7 percent— within the range, or band, set by the ERM. So trading firms made a good deal of money, having bet that the European central banks would stand behind their commitment to keep their currencies within the range specified by the ERM.

It seemed like a mistake to bet on an ERM realignment that went beyond what was permitted by the ERM's rules. But if the Italians had devalued the lire, which they said they would not do, did that not mean the emperor had no clothes? Perhaps there would be a second wave, and was it time to start selling sterling? Suddenly, in different parts of the world, investors and corporations lost faith all at once in the willingness of western European governments to permit the ERM to determine exchange rates. Speculators were eagerly trying to get out of a variety of weaker currencies, including sterling. Soros's confidence that Britain would pull the pound out of the ERM was growing.

By 1992, Soros was hardly around the New York headquarters of Soros Fund Management, which operated his Quantum Fund, the original fund he had started back in 1969. In 1988, he had turned over the day-to-day running of the fund to Stanley Druckenmiller, a young, brilliant investor who had thought the time ripe for placing a bet against the sterling. He talked to Soros about his conclusions.

Soros gave the green light, but urged his head trader to bet an even larger sum than Druckenmiller had in mind. So Druckenmiller, acting for Soros, sold $10 billion worth of sterling. There was a lot of money to be made if Soros was right about the pound being devalued. Leaving for his Fifth Avenue apartment, he seemed extremely confident.

He slept well that night. The next morning at 7:00 A.M., the phone rang at Soros's home. It was Stan Druckenmiller with terrific news. Soros heard the happy trader say that all had gone well, that George had just racked up a profit of $958 million.

When Soros's gains from other positions he took during the ERM crisis were tallied, his profit rose to nearly $2 billion. The British called September 15—the day they were forced to pull the pound out of the ERM—Black Wednesday. Soros called it White Wednesday. It was this single $10 billion bet on Britain's devaluation of the pound that made George Soros world famous. It was, and remains, his greatest coup as an investor.

He had correctly identified the instability of the European financial system, the chaos that prevailed when most others denied its existence. He was, he said gleefully, "fascinated by chaos. That's really how I make my money: understanding the revolutionary process in financial markets."

INVESTMENT SECRET

Exploit Market Overreactions

A boom/bust sequence can happen only when a market is dominated by trend-following behavior. What, though, generates trend-following behavior?

George Soros's answer is that the flawed perceptions of individual investors cause markets to feed on themselves. "Feeding on themselves" is another way of saying that investors have gotten themselves into a blind frenzy, or herdlike mentality.

Markets that feed on their own frenzy always overreact, always go to the extremes. That overreaction—pushing toward the extremes—causes a boom/bust sequence. The key to investment success, therefore, is to recognize the point at which markets begin to feed on their own momentum, for when that point is identified, the investor will then know that a boom/bust sequence is either about to begin or is already in progress.

As Soros explained:

> The reason reflexive processes follow a dialectic pattern can be explained in general terms: The greater the uncertainty, the more people are influenced by the market trends; and the greater the influence of trend-following speculation, the more uncertain the situation becomes.

The main features of a typical boom/bust sequence are:

1. The trend is as yet unrecognized.
2. Once the trend is recognized, that recognition tends to reinforce the trend and a self-reinforcing process begins. As the prevailing trend and the prevailing bias reinforce each other, the trend becomes more and more dependent on the bias. The bias grows more and more exaggerated. As the process develops, the conditions for far-from-equilibrium come into play.

3. The market's direction is successfully tested: both the bias and the trend may be tested over and over again by various outside shocks.

4. Conviction increases; if the bias and the trend survive those shocks, they are, in Soros's words, "unshakable." He calls this the period of acceleration.

5. Reality and perception diverge; a stage arises when the divergence between belief and reality is so large that one recognizes the participant as having a bias. This is the moment of truth, or the climax.

6. Ultimately, a mirror-image self-reinforcing sequence starts in the opposite direction.

The trend may continue for no other reason than inertia. But once the belief ceases to reinforce the trend, the process begins to stagnate. That loss of belief reverses the trend, and the process reaches what Soros calls a crossover point. That sets in motion an opposite direction, leading to what Soros calls a catastrophic acceleration, or crash.

In sum, Soros argues that as a trend continues, the chance for speculative transactions grows. The bias and the trend interact with one another, for as long as the trend exists, the bias becomes stronger. Once a trend is established, it will begin to run its course.

Though considered a contrarian, Soros admits that he is cautious about going against the herd. He follows the trend on most occasions, though he is always searching for the inflection point of a trend (that point where the trend changes), for that is the only time it makes sense to buck the herd.

Soros is always looking for connections that he calls "reflexive." He wrote, for example: "When people lose confidence in a currency, its decline tends to reinforce domestic inflation, thereby validating the decline. When investors have confidence in a company's management, the rise in share price makes it easier for management to fulfill investors' expectations." These connections, he notes, are at first self-reinforcing, but eventually they become self-defeating.

Soros's search, in much simpler terms, is the search for a boom/bust sequence. He found one in the real estate trust industry in the late 1960s.

In 1969 he wrote a widely circulated study in which he described the advantages of investing in a new vehicle called the real estate investment trust (or REIT). Sensing a boom/bust sequence, he compared the REIT's cycle to a three-act play, predicting correctly that REITs would first experience a boom, but then go too far and eventually collapse. Showing great prescience, he concluded that "since Act III was at least three years away, I could safely buy the shares."

He did well on the long side, selling out long before the market for REITs reached a high point. Several years later, REITs began to fall, as Soros had predicted. He at first thought it was too late to go short, but upon rereading his study, he concluded there was still time. He was right, and he earned a handsome profit. He made more than 100 percent on his money on the short side—the only time he had ever done that—because as the stocks dropped, he kept improving his short positions, using some $1 million, a good deal of money for him to risk at that time. This early exercise in testing his marketplace theories encouraged Soros immensely.

Soros's greatest profits came from detecting "self-reinforcing" moves in stocks and stock groups. Investors suddenly changed their attitude toward an industry stock group and bought heavily. A self-reinforcing phenomenon set in as the surge in stock buying reinforced the industry group's fortunes because the companies in that group boosted earnings through more borrowing, stock sales, and stock-based acquisitions.

Thus it was that the boom part of a boom/bust sequence occurred.

The game was over when market saturation and rising competition hurt the industry group's prospects and the stock became overvalued. It was a field day for short sellers when this process unraveled.

INVESTMENT SECRET

Watch for Stock Prices that Affect Fundamentals

From Soros's early explanations of his boom/bust theory, he appeared to be suggesting that market prices are influenced entirely by the bias of the participant. On occasion that bias affects not only market prices but also the so-called fundamentals. When market prices affect fundamentals, his theory of reflexivity takes on significance. This behavior—market prices affecting fundamentals—does not occur all the time. When it does occur, however, market prices do not merely reflect those fundamentals; they themselves become a fundamental that influences the fluctuation of prices.

A boom/bust process happens, Soros says, only when market prices find a way to influence the fundamentals. That happened during the conglomerate boom of the late 1960s. Soros made money during both the boom and the bust. Initially, he saw that high-tech companies were going on acquisition sprees, using their shares, which were overvalued, as currency to purchase earnings. Those earnings then justified the overvaluation. Institutional investors became impressed with the conglomerates. The high price of the conglomerates' stocks encouraged these conglomerates to buy even more companies. The misconception here was the failure of institutional investors to understand that per-share earnings growth could be manufactured by acquisitions. Soros believed that the misconception, or "bias," of these "go-go fund managers" would influence conglomerate stock prices. And indeed prices went higher, so he bought heavily. Later, he sold short and profited nicely when the decline ensued.

The conglomerate boom provided a good example of a boom/bust process because it revealed a flaw in the prevailing values of the stock. The flaw was that the values were not based purely on the fundamentals, but were reflexive. In other words, investors believed that earnings per share were independent of the market value of the shares when they were not.

The same was true during the international lending boom of the 1980s. Bankers were convinced that the debt ratios they employed to determine the borrowing capacity of debtor countries were independent of their own lending activity. Yet, in fact, their lending activity was based on their estimation of the ability of the borrower to pay off its debt. Nations thought of these debt ratios as an objective measure. In fact, the debt ratios were being influenced by the nations' own actions—if they stopped lending, the GNP dropped. Here, then, was the misconception, the failure of lenders to understand that a fundamental value was not entirely independent of the act of valuation. That misconception created the conditions for a boom/bust sequence.

This connection between the fundamentals (in this case, the debt ratio) and the value placed on those fundamentals (as influenced by the borrowing nations' actions) created a process that began as self-reinforcing—a boom period—and then deteriorated into a self-defeating one—a bust period.

What Soros found in both the conglomerate and lending cases were flawed perceptions that caused the markets to feed on themselves, to get themselves into a blind frenzy. The participants became a herd, overreacting, going to the extremes, causing a boom/bust sequence.

George Soros also found a boom/bust process in the U.S. banking system. Back in the 1930s, following the trauma of the Great Depression, banks were in a period of bust. Because they were highly regulated, they could not expand, so investors ignored bank stocks. It was a stagnant industry with little prospect of growth.

By the early 1970s, however, a new generation of bankers arose, interested in profits, slowly reaching senior positions of leadership. Their center of gravity was the First National City Bank of New York. The new breed of banks created new financial instruments and used capital more aggressively; not surprisingly, all of this was reflected in better earning performances. None of this new growth spurt impressed Wall Street, where bank shares continued to sell at little or no premium. Soros was among the first to recognize the big changes that were occurring under the surface at the banks. He sensed the misperception before most others did, a flawed belief that banks were going nowhere. In a report he wrote in 1972, he recommended the purchase of stocks of some of the more aggressively managed banks. When bank stocks began to move upward in 1972, Soros made a 50 percent profit on his position. That was the boom part of the cycle.

Soros had a good idea that enthusiasm for bank shares would collapse, but he could not predict when it would happen. It happened in 1973 when oil prices soared, as did inflation and interest rates, with the result that banks were providing only a 13 percent return on capital, too little for their shares to be sold at a premium. The bust part of the cycle had set in.

George Soros does not play the financial markets according to a set of traditional rules. That is what the other fellows do, the guys who think the world is rational and all that the world contains is rational too, including the stock market. Soros is interested in the rules of the game, but only to try to understand when those rules are about to change.

This is because, when the rules change, they might cause a reflexive relationship to begin, and that reflexivity can set off a boom/bust sequence. George Soros constantly monitors the financial markets in search of a boom/bust sequence. In knowing that financial markets are character-ized on occasion by these reflexive relationships, Soros senses that he has a leg up on the rest of the investment community.

Possessing this investment secret, however, does not guarantee that Soros always earns profits. Sometimes there are problems that have nothing to do with his own invest-ing talents. Sometimes they have everything to do with those talents. There are times, for instance, when reflexive processes simply do not exist. On occasion, those processes are there, but Soros cannot discover them in time.

Worst of all are the times when Soros searches for a reflexive process, thinks he has discovered one, only to find that he has misidentified it. On some occasions he decides to stake an investment position without thinking through how a certain financial market is operating—that is, whether a reflexive process is at work or not. But he is always look-ing for reflexive processes. When he discovers one and is able to exploit it, he makes large sums of money.

INVESTMENT SECRET

Invest First, Investigate Later

Let's put the theories aside, for even Soros admits that his theories help him only at times. Let's look now at the Soros style of investment, for it is his style as much as his theories that has helped him make a fortune.

Soros has a unique investing style, a combination of brainpower, guts, stoicism, and instinct. His theory of reflexivity is his Geiger counter, telling him where to look. It does not tell him precisely at what to aim, or most importantly when, but the theory provides him with a framework. Then the traits take over, instructing him with greater precision, guiding him to the spot, telling him about the timing.

Zeroing in for the kill, Soros then makes his move. He does it not in a grandiose way but by testing, probing, trying to determine whether what he thinks is right. He puts together a hypothesis, and on the basis of that he takes an investment position. Developing a hypothesis means making an assumption that a trend in a financial market has begun to occur.

As a general rule, Soros believes that whatever hypothesis has captured the imagination of investors at any given time will be wrong. That is, it will be based on some flaw in the hypothesis.

He adopted this notion when he worked side-by-side with partner Jim Rogers after founding the Quantum Fund. "We start with the assumption that the stock market is always wrong, so that if you copy everybody else on Wall Street, you're doomed to do poorly. Most Wall Street security analysts are mere propagandists for company managements, cribbing their investment reports from company reports or each other, and rarely uncover anything worthwhile."

Soros and Rogers meshed well together. "Usually, if we disagreed," Rogers explained, "we just did nothing."

Not always, however. If one felt strongly about a trade, he got his way.

"Once we worked things through," said Rogers, "it was pretty clear that the trade was either right or wrong. When we thought something through, a consensus was formed. I hate to use that word, because consensus investing is a disaster, but we almost always seemed to come together."

They prided themselves on being independent minded. Neither thought they could learn much from other Wall Street analysts, the ones who, according to Rogers, simply followed the herd. So they discarded much of what came in the mail. They selected their own stocks.

They did do a huge amount of research, subscribing to 30 trade publications, including *Fertilizer Solutions, Textile Week,* and a host of others. They perused general-interest magazines as well, spotting here or there a social or cultural trend that might prove valuable. Hundreds of companies had them on their mailing lists. Their files included records of over 1,500 American and foreign firms. Each day Rogers pored through 20 or 30 annual reports, hoping to find some interesting corporate development or the glimmering of a long-range trend.

Soros saw it as his main task to search for the flaws in investment theses. If he was, as at times he had to be, one of the herd, taking positions based on market trends, discovering the flaw was vital to him. It bothered him when he did not find a flaw. Knowing that flaw provided Soros with an important advantage over the rest of the investors in the financial markets, enabling him to search for signals that, once identified, would suggest to him that a certain market trend was coming to an end.

What Soros wants to know is whether a trend has been pushed to the point of excess. He is eternally searching for the trend's inflection point. That is the only time it's safe to go against the trend; to do so at any other time is to take an enormous risk. Once Soros believes he has identified the inflection point, he can then break away from the herd by getting rid of his investment position. At that time, he formulates a new investment thesis, based again on the belief that the herd is wrong. Soros likes to say that the herd is always following the wrong trend, but because he is willing at times to follow the herd, he seems to suggest that sometimes the herd is on the mark when it follows a certain trend.

On some occasions, it can take time to figure out a basis for asserting that a trend exists. That can be a problem for Soros, since by the time he formulates a thesis justifying the trend, the trend can be reversed by the market.

As long as Soros remains convinced that his original thesis is valid, he will not automatically abandon his position, even if he begins to lose money on it. The reason may not be one that invalidates his thesis. He may even add to his position. Of course, he's going to try to find out why he is losing money.

Soros's goal is to reach the point where he can say that the hypothesis is validated. If it is, he takes an even larger position, his degree of self-confidence determining just how big a position to take. If the hypothesis is invalidated, he does not delay. He gets out. He is always looking for a situation in which he can develop a hypothesis.

When they started the Quantum Fund, Soros and Rogers had divided the labor. Rogers was the analyst, Soros the decision maker. They followed the strategy of investing first and investigating later. Soros did the investing, and Rogers, the investigating.

Sometimes Soros would invest, then Rogers would investigate and find something wrong with the idea. Soros, though, might still keep his position. He liked those situations because he knew what the flaws were, helping him to know when to get out. Knowing there were flaws did not mean that Soros had to automatically get out of the position. It just meant that the position had to be watched carefully. If and when the idea seemed wrong, then the goal was to get out as quickly as possible.

Soros likes to say, "Invest first and investigate later." In practice, this means: Form a hypothesis, take a small position to test the hypothesis, and wait for the market to prove that one is right or wrong.

In essence, this favorite Soros strategy could be called "getting a feel" of the market. This happened sometimes during the 1980s when investor Jim Marquez worked as an aide to Soros. Soros used the technique only occasionally, and at times he did not even tell Marquez when he was employing it.

After much discussion, the two men would finally decide to take the plunge. Marquez then designed a staged effect, setting aside a certain amount of the fund for the position.

"All right," Soros said, "I want to buy $300 million of bonds, so start by selling $50 million."

"I want to *buy* $300 million," Marquez would remind Soros.

"Yes," Soros would reply, "but I want to see what the market feels like first. I want to see how I feel as a seller. If it comes very easily to me as a seller, if I can lose these bonds very easily, then I even want to be more of a buyer. But if those bonds are real hard to sell, I'm not sure I should be a buyer."

The Myths Surrounding George Soros

Myths soon arose about George Soros. The main one was that he could move markets, that a word from him about a certain commodity or currency would cause a shift in trading, that prices rose or fell because of what he said. In his seeming infallibility, many wanted to emulate him. Yet he was not infallible at all. He made mistakes, sometimes big ones.

A reporter doing a television documentary on Soros in December 1992 was impressed with Soros's seeming ability to move markets: "You invest in gold, and because you invest in gold everybody thinks they should invest in gold, and the price goes up; you write an article that questions the value of the deutsche mark and the deutsche mark goes down. You make an investment in London real estate and overnight it seems that the trend of downward prices is reversed. Should one person have that much influence?"

Enjoying the compliment, Soros adopted a modest stance. "Currently," he began, "the influence I have is exaggerated. In fact I'm pretty sure it is. And it will correct itself because people will realize"—he gives a big smile—"I'm not infallible, and you know, just as I'm currently swept up on a wave of interest, I'll be swept down."

He has so far been wrong on both counts. His influence has not been exaggerated, nor has the wave of interest in him diminished. He was once asked how it felt to be a guru, and he said he was amused. Others, though, were awestruck. No one can be that good in playing the financial markets, it is said; he must have some magical or supernatural powers. The truth is that Soros is no magician. His investment talents are unique, but they are of this earth, a rare combination of intuition, guts, and shrewd analysis. He does move markets on occasion, but largely because other investors have so much faith in his investment choices.

Still, the myths surrounding Soros help to give him an aura of invincibility, where his defeats are temporary setbacks and

The Myths Surrounding George Soros *(Continued)*

his triumphs miracles. For all that he is admired and held in awe by his colleagues on Wall Street and in London, Soros is something of an antihero to many because his financial record appears to be otherworldly, the work of a sorcerer more than a financial genius. He himself pours fuel on the fire by declaring unashamedly that as a child he thought he was God; that, even though he is a billionaire, he is greedy; and that he finds it easier to make money than to give it away.

Had he amassed his fortune as had some of the 19th-century captains of American industry, men like Rockefeller and Carnegie, had he been a leader in an industry such as oil or steel, someone more directly involved in building America and strengthening the nation's economy, Soros might hold more appeal for some. Soros, though, neither owns nor runs a major manufacturing enterprise; he has no specific power base within corporate America or the global financial community. He is, as he likes to boast, fundamentally an outsider, a man who sits on the sidelines, sizing up the players and the factors that might help or hurt those players. By his own admission, he is a critic, or as he likes to say half jokingly, the world's highest-paid critic. "I am a critic of the processes," he said. "I am not an entrepreneur who builds businesses. I am an investor who judges them. My function in the financial markets is that of a critic and my critical judgments are expressed by my decisions to buy and sell."

Yet what Soros does as an investor is no joke. The myths surrounding him became so real and his apparent clout over the financial markets so striking that Washington's politicians by 1993 were asking whether he and the entire hedge fund industry should be regulated.

If indeed a George Soros could move markets, and if a good deal of money could be made or lost by the actions of one man, was he not a danger? Should George Soros not be

The Myths Surrounding George Soros *(Continued)*

controlled? In the end, after hearing Soros testify in the spring of 1994 and drawing the conclusion that hedge funds, as Soros insisted, were no danger to the financial markets, the politicians decided against tacking on new regulations.

Soros has always pictured himself as a philosopher, not a financier. He likes to call himself a failed philosopher as a kind of reminder of what he had once tried to do, but without success. His great dream was to add to the world's store of knowledge about the way the world worked, and how human beings functioned. He was fascinated with the human mind, with human understanding, with the way people acquire knowledge and whether it was even possible to attain knowledge of anything. He asked himself the most difficult and complex questions about existence and thought that if he could discover some "truths" about the way we know something, he would be able to make a lasting contribution to humankind. As a student, he began the search for such knowledge. It drew him into the field of philosophy, and for a time he wanted to be a professor of philosophy. While he studied economics, he always seemed to be more of a visitor to that world than a permanent resident.

Studying economics, he felt cheated. He thought economists lacked practical knowledge about the way the world functioned. They dreamed big dreams, talked only about ideal situations, and made the mistake of thinking that the world was a rational place. Even at that early age, Soros knew well that the world was far more chaotic than economists suggested. As he began to work out his theories—theories of knowledge, theories of history, and in time, theories about the world of finance—he anchored his thinking in the belief that the world was highly unpredictable, thoroughly irrational—in short, hard to figure out.

Advancing those theories in an unpublished book he called *The Burden of Consciousness,* he tried in vain to formulate ideas

The Myths Surrounding George Soros *(Concluded)*

that would work on every occasion—the way theories were supposed to. As frustrated as he was about his inability to come up with theories that had practical value, he was even more frustrated by not being able to put his ideas into a readable format. Even he had a hard time fathoming what he had written sometimes. Concluding that he could no longer afford to wander aimlessly in the world of ideas, he set out to find worlds that he *could* conquer. The decision was, in one sense, easy. He had to make a living. Why not try to demonstrate to all those wrong-headed economists that he had a better sense of the way the world worked than they did?

He would make as much money as possible. He knew that the world of high finance carried the potential for great rewards. The risks, however, were high; it was no world for the faint of heart. In time, the faint of heart went on to other professions. Perhaps they enjoyed a few good years. Eventually, the strain of being responsible for other people's money got to them. The price was high, paid in lost sleep, leisure time lost, fewer friends. Soros found that he could function very well in this world. He did not let himself get flustered, although he contended that he felt the strain all the time. Yet his record suggested that he was indeed ice cool when it came to dealing with the financial markets.

INVESTMENT SECRET

Anticipate the Next Trend

Soros is constantly looking for sudden shifts in the stock market. Such shifts occur, for example, when investors have refrained from taking positions in a certain industry stock group for a long time but then decide abruptly to purchase those stocks in great quantities. In the wake of these sudden shifts, self-reinforcing moves might occur in these stocks. Soros is always keen to test his theory on these stocks, searching for these self-reinforcing moves.

Once the self-reinforcing mechanism takes over, the stock price climbs dramatically. This is wonderful for the stock group because now its companies will borrow more, acquire more, and find their earnings soaring. Unfortunately, this lasts for only a certain time and, with the onset of growing competition and market saturation, the stock becomes overpriced. The price then declines, benefiting short sellers enormously.

The trick for Soros has been to identify these abrupt shifts before anyone else does. As Jimmy Rogers put it: "We aren't as much interested in what a company is going to earn next quarter, or what 1975 aluminum shipments are going to be, as we are in how broad social, economic, and political factors will alter the destiny of an industry or stock group for some time to come. If there is a wide difference between what we see and the market price of a stock, all the better, because then we can make money."

Searching as well for foreign economies about to take a giant leap forward, Soros has sought to capitalize on foreign stock markets, asking which countries were opening their markets to foreign investment, promoting new policies for economic stabilization, or committed to market reform. Soros hoped to get a leg up by getting in at the wholesale level. "Like any good investor," said one former associate, "he was trying to buy a quarter for a nickel." If there were immature markets, as was the case in France, Italy, and Japan, Soros drew a bead on them, hoping for a 6- to 18-month jump ahead of other investors. Nothing complicated about it: Soros had simply learned the trick earlier than others.

Accordingly, he purchased Japanese, Canadian, Dutch, and French securities. During one part of 1971 the Soros Fund had a quarter of its total invested in Japanese stocks, a gamble that paid off when the fund doubled its money.

Soros and Rogers made shrewd selections of stocks. On one occasion in 1972 an acquaintance of Soros informed him that a private Commerce Department report described the growing American dependence on foreign fuel sources. Accordingly, the Soros Fund purchased large amounts of stock in oil-drilling, oil-field equipment, and coal companies. That same year Soros and Rogers foresaw the food crisis, and after purchasing stock in fertilizer, farm equipment, and grain-processing companies, earned impressive profits. A year later, in 1973 came the Arab oil boycott, which caused energy stocks to soar.

Around this time, Soros and Rogers craftily identified the U.S. defense industry as a potentially profitable source of investment. In October 1973 Israel was caught by surprise when Egyptian and Syrian armed forces launched major attacks against it. In the opening days of that war, Israel was on the defensive, suffering thousands of casualties and losing many planes and tanks. Soros concluded that if Israeli military technology was antiquated, then U.S. technology must be as well. Realizing that its hardware was obsolete, the Pentagon would have to spend large amounts of money.

This thesis had little appeal to most investors. Defense firms had lost so much money once the war in Vietnam drew to an end that financial analysts did not want to hear anything further about the defense industry for the time being. Early in 1974, however, Rogers started to focus in on the industry. A situation tailor-made for Soros and Rogers, the potential in the defense industry encouraged Rogers to travel to Washington, where he talked with Pentagon officials; he also journeyed to defense contractors elsewhere in the United States.

Soros and Rogers became even more convinced that they were right—and that others were going to miss out on something big. In mid-1974, they began scooping up defense stocks, including Northrop, United Aircraft, and Grumman. Though Lockheed seemed threatened with extinction, Soros and Rogers took a bet on that company, too, investing in the firm in late 1974.

He and Rogers had acquired one vital piece of information about these companies: They all had major contracts that would, when renewed, provide fresh earnings over the next few years. Early in 1975 the Quantum Fund began investing in firms that supplied electronic warfare equipment. Israeli air losses during the 1973 Yom Kippur War had been largely the result of the lack of sophisticated electronic countermeasures required to neutralize the Soviet-manufactured weaponry in Arab hands. Soros and Rogers took note of that. They also noted that the entire nature of the modern battlefield was changing. A whole new arsenal of modern equipment was now state of the art: sensors and laser-directed artillery shells and "smart bombs." All of this was going to cost a good deal of money.

13

INVESTMENT SECRET

Go for the Jugular

When George Soros believes that he is right about an investment, no investment position is too large. This is where he differs from other investors.

Investors are often right in their observations of market trends, but because they lack Soros's self-confidence, at a certain point they grow fearful that their investment will turn bad. They take a position in the stock market, watch the price go up and up for a few days or a few weeks—and then get cold feet. "This is too good to be true," they'll say. "I've got to get out before things change and I lose all my profit."

Soros scoffs at such thinking. The worst error an investor can commit, in his view, is not to be too bold but to be too conservative. When someone tells him how much he or she has invested in a stock, Soros asks a critical question: "Are you confident that the price will go up?"

If the answer is yes, Soros then asks, "Then why have you made such a small investment?"

In December 1984 Soros had his eye on Great Britain, which was just getting started with a major privatization drive. Three of the firms in question were British Telcom, British Gas, and the Jaguar car company. Soros knew that British prime minister Margaret Thatcher wanted each British citizen to own shares in British stocks. The way to accomplish that was for her government to underprice government-run securities.

Soros asked his associate Allan Raphael to look at Jaguar and British Telcom. Raphael's studies of Jaguar convinced him that the chairman, Sir John Egan, was doing a brilliant job, that the Jaguar was the hot new imported car for America. With the stock at 160 pence, Quantum took a position that represented 5 percent of its nearly $449 million portfolio, around $20 million. That was a large trading position for other people, but not for George Soros.

Raphael met with Soros. "I've done the research on Jaguar."

"What do you think?" Soros asked.

"I really like the way the company is performing. We'll be okay, I think, in the position we've taken."

To Raphael's shock, George Soros picked up the telephone and ordered his traders: "Buy another quarter of a million shares of Jaguar."

Raphael didn't want to spoil Soros's mood, but he felt obligated to utter a word of reservation. "Excuse me. Maybe I didn't make myself clear. I said: ' We'll be okay.'"

"Okay" apparently meant different things to Raphael and to Soros. To Raphael the phrase meant, "What we've done so far is okay. But let's not commit ourselves to anything more until we see how the land lies." To Soros it meant if you like the situation now, why not follow your instincts with all you've got?

Soros spelled it out for his associate: "Look, Allan, you tell me the company is doing a brilliant job of turning around. This is what they're going to earn on a cash-flow and earnings-per-share basis. You think the stock is going to get rerated upward. International investors are going to catch on to it. American investors are going to catch on to it. And you say the stock is going to go up."

To Soros, this was another tailor-made situation where he could test his theory of reflexivity. He sensed that the price of the stock would rise, that investor frenzy would soon take hold, propelling the stock upward even more. There was nothing in Soros's words with which Raphael could quarrel.

"Yeah," he agreed, "the stock is definitely going to go up."

"Buy more." Soros was adamant.

Though Raphael had said "yeah," he really wondered whether Soros really knew what he was doing.

"If the stock goes up," Soros went on, "you buy more. You don't care how big the position gets as part of your portfolio. If you get it right, then build."

Soros smiled and then said, to indicate that he wasn't interested in debating the point, "Next." He had confidence that Jaguar and British Telcom were sure bets. He had already sensed that much more was at play than the balance sheets of these companies. What was really at play was the single, crucial fact that Margaret Thatcher was going to make sure that British privatization would be underpriced.

Raphael was in mild shock. He was concerned that Soros was betting the store. He need not have worried. Quantum's profit on Jaguar was $25 million.

Another example of Soros's going for the jugular occurred on September 22, 1985. That was when the Group of Five (the American Secretary of the Treasury James Baker and the finance ministers from France, West Germany, Japan, and Great Britain), meeting at New York's Plaza Hotel, decided that the dollar, which during the early 1980s had been very strong, was valued too high and required depreciation. Soros recognized the importance of that decision. The Plaza Accord meant that the era of freely floating exchange rates was over, replaced by a "dirty" float. Soros had taken a long position on the yen and the mark. Believing that the Plaza Accord would have a positive effect on his positions, he wanted to go for the jugular, so he increased his investment. The profits poured in.

Soros took a similar attitude soon after Stanley Druck-enmiller began to work at Quantum in 1988. Druckenmiller, who had taken over the day-to-day operations for Soros, had been unenthusiastic about the dollar, so he took a large short position against the German mark. The position began to go in his favor and he was quite pleased with himself.

Soros dropped into his office and discussed the trade with him. "How big a position do you have?" he asked.

"One billion dollars," Druckenmiller answered.

"You call that a position?" Soros said, a question that has become part of Wall Street folklore. Soros persuaded Druckenmiller to double his position, and, just as Soros had predicted, even more profits poured into Quantum.

"Soros has taught me," noted Druckenmiller, "that when you have tremendous conviction on a trade, you have to go for the jugular. It takes courage to be a pig. It takes courage to ride a profit with huge leverage. As far as Soros is concerned, when you're right on something, you can't own enough."

The classic example of Soros's courage was his $10 billion bet in September 1992 that Britain would be forced to devalue the pound. Stan Druckenmiller gets credit for first calling attention to the likelihood that Britain would have to devalue. Advising Soros that he wanted to take a position against the pound, Druckenmiller listened as Soros tried to find out how confident he was. Druckenmiller said he was quite sure.

Then go for the jugular, Soros advised.

This is a once-in-a-lifetime chance, Soros suggested. The risk–reward relationship is very favorable, and Quantum should play the position on a larger scale than normal. Druckenmiller took Soros's advice. So Soros was responsible for the degree of leverage that the Quantum Group of Funds used, although the actual decision to go short on sterling was Druckenmiller's.

So Druckenmiller, acting for Soros, sold $10 billion worth of sterling. When on September 15, 1992, Britain devalued the pound, Soros was proven right and he racked up a profit of $958 million.

The most significant lesson Soros had taught him, Stanley Druckenmiller suggested, was "that it's not whether you're right or wrong that's important, but how much money you make when you're right and how much you lose when you're wrong. The few times that Soros has ever criticized me was when I was really right on a market and didn't maximize the opportunity."

INVESTMENT SECRET

Listen to World Financial Leaders

By studying George Soros's financial theory, one gets only a partial glimpse into his trading secrets. Soros admits as much—that intellectual analysis gets one only so far. After that, instinct has to take over. He admits that success as a trader does not validate his theory, that it is not a scientific proof. There must be something else.

Indeed there is. Soros's theory provides a framework, explaining how he believes that financial markets operate. It does not, however, reveal how George Soros operates. Those are the secrets that Soros keeps close to his chest.

Because Soros's theory does not provide *all* of the clues to his achievements, one might be tempted to argue that he has just been plain lucky. That is to say, he has what is known as a gambler's instinct, and over the long run, that instinct has paid off handsomely.

Few serious analysts put much credence in this explanation, however. Soros is no gambler, as one of his most veteran associates, Robert Miller, a senior vice president at Arnhold & S. Bleichroeder, notes: "If he thinks that a situation is right, he'll make an investment of it, because he's not really looking at it as gambling. Not at all. He's looking at it as an economic scenario. And whatever that economic scenario is—if the British pound is overvalued in relation to the rest of the European currencies, for example—he makes an economic decision. I wouldn't say it's gambling at all."

So it's more complicated than just rolling the dice and hoping for snake eyes.

How Soros operates is a function of a whole set of abilities, the combination of which may be unique.

There is, for example, his sheer brainpower. While others in the market are struggling to keep up with following one stock, one industry group, or one commodity, Soros takes in at any given time entire macroeconomic themes involving complex global trading scenarios.

Unlike most others, he discerns trends and movements and rhythms growing out of the public statements of world financial leaders and out of the decisions these leaders make.

What Soros understands better than most are the cause-and-effect relationships in the world's economies. If A happens, then B must follow, and C after that. This is nothing to be scoffed at. Indeed, it is one of the key trading secrets behind Soros's success.

Some have accused Soros of having some nefarious skill that is augmented by his many contacts around the world. The man has friends. Not exactly a crime, the critics are quick to admit. But those friends are in high places. Again, they are quick to concede, not exactly an act that could send someone to jail. Still, the appearance of something sinister lurking behind Soros's old-boy network ties remains strong in some people's minds.

The *Observer*, for example, referred to Soros's close ties with Jimmy Goldsmith, the takeover artist, and Nils O. Taube, Lord Rothschild's chief investment officer: "These kinds of connections, this impression of an insiders' gang, are what make more mainstream investors occasionally raise an eyebrow where Soros is concerned. His associates may talk about a sixth sense, but even some of their comments contribute to the impression that Soros has created for himself a comprehensive network for gathering information."

And yet, what was really wrong with having friends—in the right places?

Gary Gladstein, business manager for Soros Fund Management, was quite pleased to explain guru Soros's ability to pick up on macroeconomic trends anywhere in the world by pointing to the man's wide constellation of

friends. "George has friends who are intellectuals, a vast
network of contacts all over the world. He will come into
the office and say, 'I'm interested in country A, call X . . . '
And he has relied on independent advisers all over the world
throughout his career. You should see his address book."

INVESTMENT SECRET

Know When to Fold 'Em

One key to George Soros's investment success has been his skill at surviving as an investor. Surviving is such a crucial part of anyone's investing strategy that it may seem almost prosaic to even mention it. Yet it is important to pay special attention to Soros's attitude toward the subject, for it seems at first blush to be a great paradox in his case. Is not Soros the classic risk taker? Does he not encourage others to go for larger and larger positions? Is he not the king of leverage?

Of course he is all of those. Yet recalling how fragile his life was during World War II has instilled in Soros a sense of caution about the investment world, which is part and parcel of his investment bag of tricks.

In his 1987 book *Alchemy of Finance*, he writes:

> When I was an adolescent, the Second World War gave me a lesson that I have never forgotten. I was fortunate enough to have a father who was highly skilled in the art of survival, having lived through the Russian revolution as an escaped prisoner of war. Under his tutelage the Second World War served as an advanced course at a tender age ... The investment vehicle I created a quarter of a century later drew heavily on skills I learned as an adolescent.

Operating a hedge fund tested his training in survival to the maximum.

> Using leverage can produce superior results when the going is good, but it can wipe you out when events fail to conform to your expectations. One of the hardest things to judge is what level of risk is safe. There are no universally valid yardsticks: each situation needs to be judged on its own merit. In the final analysis you must rely on your instincts for survival.

Others identified the same trait, employing slightly different language, when asked to explain what accounts for Soros's investment feats. "What differentiates George," suggested Allan Raphael, who worked with him in the 1980s, "is that you have to know your own limitations." In practical terms, the art of survival for Soros meant not so much knowing when he was right about a stock as admitting when he was wrong. It meant getting out of an investment position too early rather than too late, and not being overly concerned about behavior that others might see as erratic.

Soros's survival instinct, to James Marquez, an investor who has worked with both Soros and Michael Steinhardt, forces Soros into that erratic behavior. "He'd be the first one to tell you that sometimes his actions . . . look like the most rookie, odd-lot, wrong-way kind of thing, selling at the lows, and buying at the highs. As it was he made the low in the stock market in 1987 by selling futures. But it's much easier to understand in light of what his avowed mission is: To be able to come and fight another day. He says: 'I don't want to wake up broke.'"

For instance, at the time of the October 1987 stock market crash he made sure that he did not wake up broke. On the Wednesday before the Black Monday (October 19, 1987), Soros was speaking at the John F. Kennedy School of Government at Harvard, talking about his boom/bust theory. Emerging from the meeting, he discovered the market had sold off securities in large amounts. He wished he had been in the office, selling off himself. He had seen trouble ahead, but he thought it would arise in Japan first, so he had taken short positions in the Japanese financial market. But the U.S. stock market, where he had taken long positions, fell apart first. His short positions in Japan proved a hardship, forcing him to get rid of his long positions in the United States. Wanting to avoid a margin call, he pulled out of the

Japanese market quickly. He was adhering to one of his
sacred principles: make sure you survive, worry about making money later. (He still wound up 1987 14 percent ahead
of the previous year.)

In hindsight, it appears that Soros got out of some
investment positions too early during the market collapse,
but to Jim Marquez, that behavior was classic George Soros,
giving up the battle so that he could live to fight another
day. While Soros absorbed heavy losses, by getting out when
he did he was able to prevent even worse erosions in his
positions. "It's hard for a lot of people to accept that kind
of an outcome," suggested Marquez. "And yet Soros is able
to do it because he does have enough confidence that he
will be able to come back. And of course he did, and his
greatest success came post-1987. I guess there's a message
in that for all of us."

All this talk of survival makes George Soros sound like
a conservative when it comes to playing the financial markets. If he is so cautious, how does one reconcile that caution with the reputation he and other hedge fund kings have
carved out as risk takers? Easily. The greatest of risk takers
often seem wild and reckless, but they are, in fact, the most
prudent, cautious folks around. They have to be—to stay
in the game.

A corollary to the Soros attitude toward survival is
Investment Secret 16.

INVESTMENT SECRET

Accept Your Mistakes

George Soros says that while recognizing that he may be wrong about investment positions makes him insecure, it keeps him alert as well, making him ready to correct his errors. Some believe that being mistaken about the way the financial markets will behave is shameful. To Soros, it may not be a source of pride, but it's all part of the game, and certainly not shameful. In that sense, he is like the baseball player who hits .300 and feels great about his accomplishments, even though 7 out of every 10 times he went to bat, he did not get a hit! Or he's like the scientist who knows that the path toward some great discovery is usually strewn with countless failures.

Because Soros accepts that imperfect understanding is part of the human condition, he refuses to have a negative attitude toward failing or making a mistake. What is shameful, he argues, is not being wrong but not correcting one's mistakes when they become apparent.

Soros likes to boast that what distinguishes him from the rest of the investment pack is not that he's right so much of the time and others are not, but rather that he is better at detecting when he's made a mistake than most others are. Indeed, one of his favorite investment strategies is to keep checking whether he is wrong about a certain investment position. He's always establishing and then testing investment hypotheses in the hope of discovering whether the actual course of events is matching his expectations about the way the market will behave. If those events do not match what he expects to happen, he realizes he's made a mistake. Based upon his probes, he tries to find out what has gone wrong with his calculations. Once he thinks he knows, he may be forced to modify his thesis—or discard it completely, though he does not like to change the thesis just because circumstances have changed. After all, those circumstances may be merely temporary, and may not signal a real change. Soros will try to find out what, if any, new element has entered the picture that may be impacting upon his investment position. He is not keen on getting rid of a position just because things have not gone his way. The last thing he advocates doing is to sit still and ignore a negative turn of events. What is critical is to keep watching, keep monitoring, keep examining—so that when things do occur that affect the financial position, he is alert and ready to try to understand what is happening.

17

INVESTMENT SECRET

Don't Bet the Ranch

Part of the art of survival for Soros has been learning never to risk everything. That was the main lesson George Soros learned from his father: that it is all right to take risks, but when taking risks, don't bet the ranch.

Hiding from the Nazis, as he did for a year during 1944, George Soros had no choice but to risk everything. When he used false identity papers, he knew that exposure meant death. Later, in his business career, he had more latitude. He did not have to make life-or-death choices. He could take risks without having to worry that failure might cost him his life. Risk taking might at times even be pleasant—as long as he left himself room to recover.

"I'm very concerned with the need to survive," Soros told a television interviewer at the height of his success in 1992, "and not to take risks that could actually destroy me."

Moreover, going to the brink in an investment was not something that good investors did. Any employee of Soros who practiced such high-stakes gambling was quickly reined in. Yet Soros admits that going to the brink in taking an investment position can have a purpose in that it can focus one's mind. It can help someone to think clearly about how the financial markets are behaving. Soros even suggests that taking risks is critical to him, that it gets his adrenaline going. Danger stimulates him. Not that he loves danger. But he needs to feel that he is fully engaged in the market, to play the game to the hilt.

Never bet the ranch, Soros says, but never stand idly by when there's money to be made either.

INVESTMENT SECRET

Study, Pause, Reflect

For Soros, the game is often fought over the long term, for the effects of interest rate and currency changes can take time and sometimes require much patience. Soros has the patience that other investors often lack. As Soros has suggested "To be successful, you need leisure. You need time hanging heavily on your hands."

Byron Wien, a close associate, sensed this character trait in Soros, a kind of "laid-back" approach to life and to finances.

"He feels," said Wien, "that he should not be dependent upon other people. Some people spend all day talking to brokers. He doesn't feel that's the way to spend your time. Instead, he prefers to talk to a few people who can really be helpful and to think and read and reflect. He looks for somebody who has a kind of philosophical sensitivity. He's not interested solely in people who have made a lot of money . . . without any soul. He doesn't feel he has to do that in the office.

"He . . . once said something to me that was very useful: 'The trouble with you, Byron, is that you go to work every day and you think that because you go to work every day you should do something. I don't go to work every day. I only go to work on the days that make sense to go to work . . . And I really do something on that day. But you go to work and you do something every day and you don't realize when it's a special day.'"

INVESTMENT SECRET

Endure the Pain

George Soros admits that he hates to lose money. The worst thing one can do when losing money is to suppress one's feelings. Of course embarrassment and anger are natural responses to losing money. You will want to bury your mistakes, not make them public. Your reputation is at stake. Your clients' money is dwindling.

Keeping your reactions to loss to yourself, says Soros, only makes it worse. You have to know how to endure such losses, how to suffer such pain. Otherwise, you can't play for the long haul. In short, you have to be cool and detached, unafraid to talk with others about the losses. There's comfort in finding out that others have absorbed losses and remained in the fray.

Every day you are taking risks. That is part of the pain, for you know that at some point you might face serious losses. If you're not prepared for the pain, says Soros, get out of the game. Don't entertain thoughts of staying in it for the long haul. If you want to be a player, stay cool.

Soros is the model stoic. His example is worth following. Being a stoic takes guts. How else to explain the dispassionate manner in which Soros buys and sells in numbers that defy the imagination. He himself would deny that he possesses much courage, for he would say that the key to investing is to know how to survive. Survival at times means playing the game conservatively, cutting losses when necessary, always keeping a large portion of assets out of play.

Others dealing in decisions affecting hundreds of millions of dollars would shake in their boots and lose sleep. With his nerves of steel, Soros plays with high stakes.

While others let their egos sometimes get in the way of making intelligent market decisions, Soros understands that the wise investor is the dispassionate investor. It makes no sense to claim infallibility. It does no good to reprove oneself when a stock shifts in the wrong direction. It is better to admit having made a mistake—and get out of the position.

One day in 1974 Soros was playing tennis with an acquaintance when the phone rang. It was a broker in Tokyo calling, letting Soros in on a secret. This was the time of Watergate, and President Richard Nixon was knee deep in the scandal that was to bring him down later in the year. The broker was calling to let Soros know that the Japanese were reacting poorly to Nixon's difficulties.

Having taken heavy positions in the Japanese stock market, Soros had to decide what to do—stay in, or get out? His tennis partner noticed that sweat that had not been there during the match had formed on Soros's forehead. Yet it did not take Soros more than a fraction of a second to decide. He gave orders to sell. He did not hesitate or feel that he needed to consult anyone before taking such a large step. Armed with tremendous self-confidence, Soros had no regrets about what he did. He might have sweated for a short while, but that was undoubtedly from the tennis, not from the investment decision he had just made.

Allan Raphael, who worked with Soros in the 1980s, believes that Soros's stoicism has been of inestimable value to the investor. It is a trait that few others have, he asserts. "You can count them on one hand. When George is wrong, he gets the hell out. He doesn't say, 'I'm right, they're wrong.' He says, 'I'm wrong,' and he gets out, because if you have a bad position on, it eats you away. All you do is think about it—at night, at your home. It consumes you. Your eye is off the ball completely. This is a tough business. If it were easy, meter maids would be doing it. It takes an inordinate amount of discipline, self-confidence, and basically lack of emotion."

George Soros: Who Is He?

Though small in stature, Soros looks rugged and athletic.
He has cropped, wavy hair and wears wire-rimmed glasses.
Some say he looks like either an economics professor or a
ski instructor. His English, while excellent, is spoken with
a slight trace of a Hungarian accent. One writer described
him as "an intense, squarely built man with a wrinkled brow,
an angular chin, and a thin mouth. His hair is cut *en brosse*.
He has a flat, slightly harsh voice." Another said: "His relaxed
air and lilting Hungarian accent lend him the style of a European grandee. His forehead is furrowed, suggesting hours
spent pondering the state of the world—an impression of
scholarship which he is eager to encourage." To a writer for
The Observer, Soros seemed to fit right into the European
mold. "He is [an] . . . elegant man stamped with the indeli-
ble courtliness and restrained irony of Austro-Hungarian
café society. In an earlier age one could easily have imagined him sipping his mocha over chess with Trotsky in the
old Café Central in Vienna."

The Independent, the British newspaper, summed up Soros's
appearance this way: "He is no glitzy Gordon Gekko, antihero of that quintessentially eighties movie, *Wall Street*. He
looks a decade younger than his years, perhaps as a result
of his compulsive tennis playing and lack of interest in the
flashy lifestyle that New York offers to the seriously rich.
He neither drinks nor smokes, and his taste in food is modest. He comes across like an earnest, rather untidy Middle
European professor."

Money, as it turns out, has had only marginal appeal for
George Soros.

He did not set out to be a world-class investor making
huge amounts of money. He yearned instead to be a man of
ideas and always found the realm of the intellect more
appealing than that of finance. Yet a good deal of money
came to him easily. Perhaps that is why he felt tainted by it,

George Soros: Who Is He? *(Continued)*

although in his view, speculation was not immoral, nor was it simply another form of gambling. To those who assailed him for ganging up on the financial markets, Soros made no excuses for his incredible financial record. He liked to say that if he were not raking in the money, someone else would. Yet, at some point, he decided that he had more money than he needed to live comfortably.

By the late 1970s and early 1980s, Soros found the pain associated with investing too severe. It was the pain that came from running an investment fund that had gotten far larger than he ever imagined; it was also the pain that came from being in the game for so long and worrying about every investment.

He was a survivor. He had learned that art from his father, and he had practiced it during World War II, hiding from the Nazis during 1944 in Budapest. To survive in the financial markets sometimes meant beating a hasty retreat. That is what Soros did in the early 1980s. He adopted a low profile and let others handle the fund. He also came to a major conclusion. He wanted something more of life than the investment world. He wanted to do something with his money that would be useful. He yearned to make a contribution—not just any contribution, but one that would be remembered.

It was not that he totally abhorred money. On the contrary, he acknowledged that he had an acquisitive streak in him: "I still consider myself selfish and greedy. I am not putting myself forward as any kind of saint. I have very healthy appetites and I put myself first."

Once he determined *how* to spend his money, he was free to just go ahead and spend it. He had no need to consult any board of directors or family members. With that kind of freedom, he wanted to make sure he chose wisely.

Eventually, he focused on his native Hungary and its surroundings in eastern Europe and later, the former Soviet

George Soros: Who Is He? *(Continued)*

Union, as the target for his philanthropy. Soros had left Hungary years earlier because he could not tolerate the political systems prevalent there—first fascism in World War II, then communism in the postwar years. The "closed" societies that had developed throughout eastern Europe and in the Soviet Union were offensive to him. To him the model political system was one that maximized political and economic freedom, the kind that happened to exist in the United States and in western Europe.

He was drawn to the challenge of making a dent in those closed societies. His goal became to spread his largesse over these vast areas—and make a difference. Others—routinely western governments, sometimes private foundations—tried to influence these closed societies, to woo them to western ideals and values. Never, however, had a private individual from the West sought to westernize these countries. Soros believed he was up to the challenge. Just as he had taught himself to do with his investments, he decided to begin slowly, monitor his progress prudently, and spend his money carefully. To have an impact without arousing suspicion would be difficult; to win the approval of the political authorities for his efforts might be impossible. He wanted, however, to give it a try.

Just getting a toehold in some of these countries was an achievement, given the suspicions and hostilities of the governments. In time, though, Soros Foundations blossomed in most of the countries of eastern Europe and in the former Soviet Union. By the mid-1990s, Soros was giving hundreds of millions of dollars away, becoming the most important private western donor between the Danube and the Urals. Praised by many as a saint, damned by cynics as an intruder, Soros had finally found a way to make a difference, gain some respect, and do something outside the precincts of Wall Street and the City of London. The philanthropy aimed

George Soros: Who Is He? *(Concluded)*

at opening up closed societies had given him far more satisfaction than accumulating all that money. It also had given him far more exposure.

He liked the publicity; indeed he was eager for it, because he wanted the world to know that he was not simply the Man Who Broke the Bank of England. He believed, too, that the publicity could help him in his aid efforts. Yet he was not entirely content, sensing that he would be expected to lay bare his secretive world of investment in the process.

He wanted publicity, but only positive publicity. He yearned to be on the front page of the *New York Times* but not in a role that made him seem like a suspicious, shadowy figure whose clout in the financial world was as monumental as it was unclear. If he preferred to be a private figure, that was no longer possible. He was too visible, his accomplishments too substantial, his reach too vast. Others wanted to know much more about him even though there was a good deal he did not want to tell.

INVESTMENT SECRET

Exercise Discipline

George Soros has a practical attitude toward financial markets that few others have. He also has a certain discipline. As Byron Wien, U.S. investments strategist at Morgan Stanley, notes:

> He understands the forces that influence stock prices. He understands there is a rational and irrational side of markets. And he understands that he isn't right all the time. He is willing to take vigorous action when he is right and really take advantage of an opportunity, and to cut his losses when he's wrong. That's a characteristic a lot of people don't have. A lot of us are right a lot of the time, but we don't trust our bets as hard as he does because we're afraid. He has great conviction when he's sure that he's right as he was in the sterling crisis in 1992.

Part of Soros's instinct is picking up on when there is movement, one way or the other, in the stock market. This is not something one can learn in school; it was not part of the economics courses he took as an undergraduate at the London School of Economics in the early 1950s. This is a psychological gift, and Soros has it. Edgar Astaire, his London partner, has no trouble defining the Soros touch: "His greatest key to success is his psychology. He understands the herd instinct. He understands when lots of people are going to go for something, like a good marketing man."

Soros has self-confidence, but it comes not simply from following his own instincts. He wants also to know what others think. Allan Raphael recalls: "He always wanted you to hear the other side of an argument. If you liked something, he wanted you to talk to someone who didn't like it. He always wanted an intellectual rub there. He always rethinks a position. You always have to rethink it and rethink it and rethink it. Things change. The prices change. Conditions change. It was up to you as a fund manager to constantly rethink your position."

A typical dialogue between Soros and Raphael would go like this:

Raphael: "This position is working out."

Soros: "Do you think you should be selling some here?"

Raphael: "No."

Soros: "You want to buy some more?"

Back and forth, reviewing the positions.

"Soros," said Allan Raphael, "has an incredible ability to ask the right questions. Then he'll look at the charts and he'll go okay."

When the time is ripe for a decision, it never takes him more than 15 minutes of study.

Fund managers like Raphael have had some flexibility—not everything has to go through Soros. Small positions of, say, $5 million, can be built without a Soros okay. "But," noted Raphael, "it was really to your benefit to talk to him about it because he was smart."

INVESTMENT SECRET

Hedge Your Bets

To understand how George Soros makes his money, it is important to appreciate that he plays in the right ball park.

That "ball park" is hedge funds, where the profits are potentially the highest among all who play the investment game. Soros was among the first in the hedge fund field and among the first to use a current favorite instrument of the hedge funds known as financial derivatives, which include futures, options, and swaps.

The phrase *hedge fund* means different things to different people. What is a hedge fund?

Aficionados argue that they should be called "hedged funds," though very few use that name. Hedge funds were created by Alexander Winslow Jones in 1949. Noting that some parts of an economy did well while others did poorly, Jones devised a scale of investing. A very bullish investor might go long with 80 percent of his positions and short the other 20 percent. A very bearish investor might short 75 percent of his positions and go long the other 25 percent. What was important for the investor was to vary the level of the portfolio's risk.

Jones began quietly, and not much occurred in the hedge fund arena for another 15 years. In 1957, however, Warren Buffett began his own highly successful hedge fund. At first, hedge funds invested only in stocks buying and selling similar securities, hoping for an overall gain. In time, though, the surviving hedge funds looked around for other opportunities. Eventually they found them. In the mid-1960s the media focused attention on some hedge funds, but interest diminished after 1970, and many investors folded in the bear market of 1973–1974.

Opportunities for investors broadened as a result of the 1971 decision to allow exchange rates to float. By the mid-1980s currency options and futures were used to a greater degree, and interest in hedge funds revived by the mid-1980s. Before 1985, the central banks of the industrialized countries adopted a hands-off approach toward exchange rates. What spurred the growth of the hedge funds—especially in the late 1980s and early 1990s—and the rise of George Soros to world-class investor status—was a decision by European banks in 1985 to lower the value of the dollar in order to increase American exports by making them cheaper. As a result of the devaluing of the dollar, the incentive to trade currencies grew, and Soros and other hedge fund traders took advantage. After 1985, global currency trading intensified. Between 1986 and 1989, it doubled to $40 billion daily, according to a survey by the Bank for International Settlements. Compare that with the amount of daily trading in U.S. Treasury bonds, which amounts to only $30 billion, and U.S. stocks, which is less than $10 billion.

When world currency traders took on Europe's central banks and engineered the September 1992 coup against the pound, it was the first indication of the great power the hedge funds had amassed. It was not the stock players or investment bankers who were raking in large profits but hedge fund kings.

A good deal of secrecy surrounds hedge funds. They cherish their privacy and are not pleased with the prospect of others learning too much about how they function. Most of Soros's activities are not even known to his shareholders, since his funds do not have any reporting obligations.

The hedge funds—dubbed by *The Wall Street Journal* "Wall Street's newest great casino"—are the largest and least regulated of the financial markets, dominating high finance. As much as $500 billion is invested in the nearly

1,000 hedge funds now in operation. (Soros's fund has had as much as $13 billion of that at times.) That is a hefty portion of the $3.5 trillion of investment capital spent in the market each year. Each day hedge funds trade an estimated $75 billion, more than eight times the value of the shares traded on the New York Stock Exchange.

Those who run the funds became by 1994 the most powerful, best-compensated businesspeople in the country, rivaling the trading power of Wall Street's most important firms. They were, in the words of *Business Week*, the "gunslingers of the investment world—unregulated, freewheeling and often far better as investors than their conventional counterparts."

From 1987 to 1990, the median hedge fund was up 75.1 percent a year—that compared to just 35.1 percent for the median mutual fund and 56.2 percent for the S&P 500. In 1992 alone, average hedge fund returns were about three times the S&P 500. Soros, Julian Robertson, and Michael Steinhardt did far better. The best evidence of how well the hedge funds were doing came from gazing at *Financial World*'s list of the top money earners for 1993.

Those on the list made more money cumulatively than others on previous lists had. Roughly half of those on the list either ran or worked for hedge funds. Hedge fund managers occupied the first five positions; Soros headed the list with an income of $1.1 billion, the first American to earn over $1 billion in a year. Hedge fund managers also held eight of the top ten slots, and accounted for 46 of the 100 on the list.

Number two was Julian Robertson, who earned $500 million; number three, Michael Steinhardt, $475 million; and, incredibly, number four, Stanley Druckenmiller, George Soros's right-hand man, at least $210 million. Of the 100 on the list, 9 were Soros people.

At the time the survey was taken, Soros had more than $11 billion under management; Robertson, $6 billion; and Steinhardt, more than $4 billion. Each receives a 1 percent fee for managing those assets plus 20 percent of the portfolio's appreciation, although Soros takes 15 percent.

To make those profits, the hedge fund kings posted whopping returns by playing the global trend toward lower interest rates. They bought foreign bonds, especially in Europe and Japan, often in the futures market. They bet correctly on how various currencies would react to sliding interest rates. Many played the boom in the markets of the emerging world.

No wonder, then, that hedge funds were becoming so popular. More than 800 had appeared by the early 1990s, double the number of a few years earlier.

22
INVESTMENT SECRET

Keep a Low Profile

Wall Street has always been entranced with people who can make things happen, who appear to have a superior grasp of how high finance works. In the past it was a Morgan or a Stanley, a Gould or a Baruch. In the early 1990s, it was George Soros and the other hedge fund champions.

According to James Grant, editor of *Grant's Interest Rate Observer* in New York, these Wall Street titans often had far less financial clout than was ascribed to them, yet the Street seemed more comfortable believing that someone or some institution could control things, could make things happen. "I look on Soros as one of these figures, partly mythical, partly real," Grant observes. "People have to project their anxieties and resentments and envy on something animate. They want to think that somebody is making markets happen. They can't believe that supply and demand are actually doing that, that markets personally discount future events. They want to believe there is a Soros.

". . . In a bear market that person could be the fall guy but in any case I think people do like to believe that somebody has succeeded, somebody is responsible, somebody can be reached on the phone, somebody can be subpoenaed.

"I think hedge funds today are 'them.' The 'they' that people have always talked about are today the hedge funds. They move massive amounts of money at the speed of light. They do so with audacity—until recently with brilliant success. George Soros, Julian Robertson, Leon Cooperman, and Paul Tudor-Jones, that ilk, together they constitute 'them.'"

How easy is it to become one of "them," to join a hedge fund?

Not easy at all. Nor, for many investors, would it be very wise, for hedge funds carry high risk and require access to a good deal of money.

The Securities and Exchange Commission, which oversees the U.S. financial markets, obligates investors in American hedge funds to have either a net worth of $1 million or an annual income of at least $200,000 for two consecutive years, $300,000 for a couple. Most fund managers insist that their investors be even wealthier. To qualify for membership in the Quantum Fund, one needed to come up with $1 million.

Quantum investors, moreover, cannot be U.S. citizens or residents. This is because the funds, which are domiciled in the Netherlands Antilles or the British Virgin Islands, are not registered with the Securities and Exchange Commission. This permits them more operating flexibility and freedom from U.S. disclosure rules. That offshore status means that although these funds may be able to influence entire markets, they can avoid much U.S. governmental regulation.

A myth has grown up that hedge funds are totally unregulated. That is not the case, for the SEC Act of 1934 requires investment managers of funds over $100 million to file information with the SEC. Hedge fund managers are also subject to antifraud legislation. Hedge funds can avoid registering as an investment firm, however, by limiting the number of investors to under 100 and by offering their products as private placements. One major difference between Soros's offshore fund and the U.S. hedge funds concerns taxes. The shareholders in offshore funds do not have to pay taxes on capital gains as long as a majority of the fund's shareholders are not Americans.

In some cases Americans can invest in these offshore funds, but they do not qualify for the favorable tax treatment. To simplify things, however, most offshore funds ban—or, at a minimum, discourage—U.S. investors.

As for George Soros, he worked it out so that he, a U.S. citizen since 1961, became an exception to the rule. Despite being a U.S. citizen, he was able to qualify for his own off-shore fund. Most of the Soros fund's investors are European.

It has been in Soros's interest to have the financial community believe he is just another investor. We know and he knows that he is not. But he has worked hard at convincing others that he's just a small-time trader whose positions, because they are so small, cause no real harm to the investment world.

Accordingly, Soros has became a kind of spokesman for hedge funds. It may seem an odd role for someone so eager to conceal his investment strategies. Yet it is not so odd when one keeps in mind that Soros reveals very few of his secrets. He simply beats the drums for hedge funds and defends themselves against all comers. Now and again he even urges more regulation for hedge funds.

In Bonn, for example, on March 2, 1994, Soros declared that it would be legitimate for central banks to consider regulating the giant hedge funds. "I feel that there is an innate instability in unregulated markets," Soros told reporters. "I think that it behooves the regulators to regulate.

"I do believe that markets without regulation are subject to crashing and therefore it is a very legitimate issue for [central banks] to investigate. We are ready to cooperate with them on it. I just hope that whatever regulations they introduce do not do more harm than good."

When he was asked to comment on charges that hedge funds increase market volatility and instability, Soros replied: "I would say that markets have a tendency to overshoot and so I don't believe in the perfect market at all. Therefore, I don't think that hedge funds are perfect either, otherwise they wouldn't lose 5 percent in a day."

Meeting in Basle that month, the central bank governors from the Group of Ten industrialized nations came up with no reason to write new regulations for hedge funds or banks that used their own capital to trade on the international markets. The markets had corrected themselves following the early year's turmoil, and there was no reason to anticipate further trouble.

When he testified before the House Banking Committee in April 1994, Soros sought to convey to the committee that hedge funds should not be blamed for the plummeting prices in stocks and bonds earlier in the year. "I reject any assertion or implication that our activities are harmful or destabilizing."

Soros was asked if it was possible for a private investor like himself to amass enough capital to manipulate the value of a currency such as the Italian lire or British pound. "No," he replied. "I do not believe any market participant can, other than for a short time, successfully influence currency markets for major currencies contrary to market fundamentals . . . Hedge funds are relatively small players given the size of the global currency markets. The lack of liquidity in markets for smaller currencies also acts to prevent any investor from successfully influencing prices for a minor currency. Any investor trying to influence prices by acquiring a large position in that currency will, because of the lack of liquidity, face disastrous results when the position is sold."

Some who hear the phrase "hedge fund" for the first time may think that these funds are conservative. After all, built in to the notion of hedging is being careful. These funds, however, are anything but conservative. Rather, hedge funds adopt a strategy of betting on some investments to increase in value and others to drop in value—in effect, "hedging" against sizable market swings.

With all the excitement surrounding hedge funds in the 1990s, ordinary investors have sought out the hedge funds, hoping to join them. They are, however, essentially closed clubs, inaccessible to all but a very few. Still, there is a great deal the individual investor can learn from the way hedge fund managers like Soros operate. While the amounts of money they invest are substantially higher than that of most individual investors, their strategies can provide valuable lessons for anyone involved in the financial markets.

INVESTMENT SECRET

Use Leverage to Boost Returns

Hedge funds offer a number of attractions. For the investor with big bucks who wants to make even bigger bucks, hedge funds are just the right free-swinging vehicle. Conventional managers of mutual and pension funds use a limited array of techniques, hoping to be as conservative as possible. Hedge fund managers, unconstrained by such conservatism, employ a wide variety of techniques, the most dazzling of which is investing with borrowed money. That's called leveraging.

Hedge funds, while much in the news in the 1990s, were little known and less understood in the late 1960s. Robert Miller, a senior vice president at Arnhold & S. Bleichroeder, who worked with George Soros in those days, recalls how Soros operated then:

> If George invested in German shares, since it's a dollar-denominated fund, there are two ways of doing it. The first would be to buy German marks to pay for the shares that you bought. This meant that you would have a currency exposure because you would be long German securities which you would then be selling for marks. And you've already bought the marks. The other way is to hedge by either borrowing German marks so that there would be no currency exposure; or by doing a foreign exchange whereby you would sell the German mark forward again to eliminate the exposure to the German mark. That is called hedging your portfolio.

Another technique the hedge funds employ with great frequency is shorting, or betting that the value of some assets will decline. A trader who shorts sells a security he or she does not own, hoping that later, when that security has to be delivered to the buyer, it can be acquired at a lower price. Soros used this technique effectively on the eve of Black Wednesday, when he shorted sterling in September 1992.

It sounds like a harmless enough technique. But to some, it has the ring of being unpatriotic. How can someone bet that a company is going to do poorly? ask the critics of shorting. What kind of American would do that, anyway? Doesn't this person have faith in the economy? What kind of person would try to exploit someone else's bad fortune?

Soros did not care about such criticism. For him the technique of shorting worked like a charm, yielding large gains in U.S. and overseas markets. His fund also leveraged itself by purchasing stock on margin. One dividend for the Quantum Fund was its small size; freed of burdensome bureaucracies, it was able to move in and out of a stock position far more easily than large firms.

Soros's play on Avon is an excellent example of his reaping benefits by going short. It was his insight, long before Avon's earnings started to plunge, that an aging population would mean far lower sales for the cosmetics industry.

Soros gleefully explained: "In the case of Avon, the banks failed to realize that the post–World War II boom in cosmetics was over because the market was finally saturated and the kids aren't using the stuff. It was another basic change that they just missed." To sell the shares short, the Quantum Fund borrowed 10,000 Avon shares at the market price of $120. Then the stock plummeted. Two years later, Soros bought the shares back at $20 each. That $100-a-share profit earned the fund $1 million.

This is the most common form of hedging. Mutual funds are prohibited from shorting by the Internal Revenue Service's so-called short-sale rule, which states that mutual fund companies cannot receive more than 30 percent of their gross income from selling investments held for less than three months. Short sales are considered short-term trades. Even so, a few mutual fund managers have won SEC approval to sell short.

One of Wall Street's leading hedge fund managers, requesting anonymity, noted that Benjamin Graham, the founding father of security analysis, had hypothesized the concept of intrinsic value, in effect what a security is worth under certain circumstances, weighing in interest rates, the state of the economy, the profits of the company, and the like. "The job of the analyst, the money manager, is to identify the security that is above the intrinsic value. So a conventional investor would sell that security whereas a hedge fund might short it and when the stock is below its intrinsic value, when it's undervalued, he would buy it. The difference between a conventional investor and a hedge fund investor is that the former might buy it for cash and the latter might buy it at leverage and have more than 100 percent invested."

The same hedge fund operator described the brutalities of being heavily leveraged.

> It's gut-wrenching. Very intense. You have to have a special ability to deal with the leverage that George Soros or Michael Steinhardt do. The three most leveraged players out there are George Soros, Tiger (Julian Robertson) and Michael Steinhardt. It takes a certain kind of mentality, a certain confidence in one's ability to see the play because small fluctuations against you can have a very magnifying financial impact. The dollar–yen moved 4–5 percent in a day [in February 1994]. It cost Soros $600 million. We live in a world where 4–5 percent moves are not that unusual. The Federal Reserve raises its interest rates by a quarter of a point, the Dow drops 97 points. It takes a certain mentality, it takes a certain appetite for risk. It has to be done intelligently.
>
> Warren Buffett is not a leveraged player. He's a cash-basis investor. He takes large concentrated bets on individual

securities, but he uses cash. George Soros is a leveraged player. You figure that takes a certain intestinal fortitude, a certain degree of conviction in the bet, a basic set of financial controls; you have to make sure you're on top of the leverage.

Hedge funds are not only more likely than mutual funds to go long and short. They also play options, futures, and other derivatives. Hedge funds take more heavily concentrated positions and trade more frequently than mutual funds. The downside of all this for hedge funds is the added risk. The upside, if all works well, is the possibility of great profits. Because most investors in hedge funds must leave their money in the funds for a long period, their gains are usually reinvested. And so their profits pile up.

Hedge funds offer an investor the opportunity to take positions in any of the financial markets around the world. Mutual fund managers, trying to rely on their expertise in one field, often rely on one market. Moreover, mutual fund managers find the volatility associated with international financial markets too perplexing and risk laden to be attractive.

Hedge funds make a point of doing a great deal of trading. In 1988, George Soros turned his portfolio over 18 times; four years later, in 1992, 8 times.

In the 1990s, hedge funds had become the darling of the investment set, largely because of the staggering amounts of money won by the most famous of the hedge-fund managers. Leading the pack was Soros and his Quantum Fund. Others did well too, though not nearly as well as Soros. These include Michael Steinhardt of Steinhardt Partners, Julian Robertson of Tiger Fund, and Leon Cooperman of Omega Advisers, Inc.

The best-known of these hedge funds racked up returns of between 25 to 68 percent in 1992. That was well beyond the 7 to 8 percent an investor would have made in a U.S. stock-index fund. While Soros's fund was up 67.5 percent in 1992, Steinhardt's had an increase of about 50 percent, Robertson's, 27.7 percent.

However attracted by all of this an average investor may be, he or she cannot simply go out and hire a George Soros or Michael Steinhardt—and then sit back and wait for the big bucks to roll in. Hedge funds are indeed select clubs, small fraternities of sophisticated, high-net-worth investors who have a great deal of money to put at risk.

By 1994, hedge funds had become so powerful that politicians began talking about the need for new forms of regulation. They were mysterious, and whenever any institution that mysterious makes lots of money, questions are going to be raised. Fear had mounted that the large amount of money the hedge fund operators were putting into the system was affecting the financial markets. When the bond market suffered a setback in early 1994, the belief grew that hedge funds had been the cause. Hedge fund managers disputed the claim, arguing that their investment positions were far smaller than those of investment and commercial banks.

As for George Soros, his own position on regulation is paradoxical. He has every reason to oppose regulation. After all, in the absence of regulation he has made his fortune. Soros calls himself a specialist on instability, someone who lives off of the chaotic state of financial markets. Why would he want regulation? Yet he favors a centralized banking system for the international financial community. That is the paradox. "I don't hesitate to speculate in currency markets—even though I say that currency markets ought to be stabilized," he points out. "We have to distinguish between the participant and the citizen. As a participant, you play by the rules. As a citizen, you have a responsibility to try to change the system if it's wrong."

In 1992, the SEC produced a 500-page report on offshore funds. This was around the time that there was suspicion that three major hedge funds, including Quantum, had made large purchases of U.S. Treasury bonds at auctions in which Salomon Brothers of New York stood accused of trying to execute a market squeeze. Government investigators gave all three funds a clean bill of health. The SEC report came to the conclusion that the hedge funds did not need to be more closely regulated. For the time being, it appears that the hedge funds will continue to go relatively unregulated.

24

INVESTMENT SECRET

Pick the Best *and the Worst* Stocks

George Soros engages in macro analysis, the big picture, international politics, monetary policies around the globe, changes in inflation, interest rates, currencies. Jim Marquez, who worked with Soros in the 1980s as his right-hand man, remembered how Soros decided which way the "macros" were going to go, what was happening in the big picture. Marquez then had the task of looking for those industries and firms that would best take advantage of the expected new alignments in the international finance community.

If the expectation was that interest rates would rise, Soros had Marquez look for industries that would be hurt from such an expectation. Marquez would then short those stocks. Soros employed the technique of selecting two companies in an industry for investment.

When industries were identified that would benefit from higher inflation, the fund would go long. Marquez observed: "We would start at the industry level and once we got into the industry we would look for the subcomponents of the major companies that would best demonstrate those trends that we foresaw."

Once that was accomplished, Soros insisted that Marquez come up with two companies in the industry. But not just any two. One had to be the best company in the industry. As the preeminent player, this firm's stock would be the one that all the others would want to purchase first. These purchases would push the price of the stock up. Soros would go long on that stock.

The other company in which to invest would be the worst one in the industry, the most highly leveraged, the one with the worst balance sheet. It was the most undervalued and so there was a good deal of money to be made when its stock finally rose. Soros would go long on that stock too.

Once these two companies, the best and the worst, were identified, there was no need to invest in any others in that industry. In the computer industry, for example, Soros might buy stock in IBM at the same time that he would purchase stock in Data-General. IBM was, of course, the most successful company in the computer industry over the long haul. Data-General had been in business a long time but had not made nearly as much money as others in the industry, even though during the 1980s especially, the computer industry had been exploding. Data-General, however, was worth looking at because it was bound to recover once it learned to benefit from the positive experience of others in the industry. And Data-General's profit increases would be disproportionately higher compared to, say, an IBM. So Data-General's stock would eventually do very well. That was Soros's thinking.

He applied the same mental exercise to the drug industry, where he would purchase stock in Merck and at the same time go for stock in Syntex, which, back in the 1980s, was much smaller than Merck but was growing at a faster pace. Syntex, of Palo Alto, California, owed its existence to the birth control pill, though in later years it relied largely on an arthritis drug called Naprosyn, which hit the market in 1976. By the late 1980s over half of Syntex's sales and profits were coming from Naprosyn and Anaprox, a similar compound. Syntex, accordingly, carried a good deal of risk. If things went well, if Syntex were to make some new drug discoveries, the company would benefit, and its profits would soar even higher than that of a larger company. As a one-product company, however, it sold at a much smaller valuation than other companies in the industry.

Soros's technique in choosing the best and the worst stocks in an industry might seem to be, on the surface at least, an excellent example of hedging. Yet Soros was not really engaged in hedging. He believed that both the best and the worst stocks would do well. That was why he focused on them and not on any others in the industry.

INDEX